LINDA BOZZO

Amazing Animal Feet

PowerKiDS
press™

New York

To my family and friends and all of your amazing features that make you who you are.
—LBS

Published in 2008 by The Rosen Publishing Group, Inc.
29 East 21st Street, New York, NY 10010

First Edition

Editor: Joanne Randolph
Book Design: Kate Laczynski
Photo Researcher: Nicole Pristash

Photo Credits: Cover © www.istockphoto.com/Scott Leigh; pp. 5, 9, 11, 13, 15, 17, 19, 21 Shutterstock.com; p. 7 © www.istockphoto.com/Kitch Bain.

Library of Congress Cataloging-in-Publication Data

Bozzo, Linda.
  Amazing animal feet / Linda Bozzo. — 1st ed.
      p. cm. — (Creature features)
  Includes index.
  ISBN 978-1-4042-4167-1 (library binding)
  1. Foot—Juvenile literature. I. Title.
  QL950.7.B69 2008
  591.47'9—dc22
                                    2007025845

Manufactured in the United States of America

CONTENTS

All animals have special **features**. These features can help them stay alive in their **habitats**. For some animals feet are important tools. Ducks have **webbed** feet that make them strong swimmers. Orangutans use their feet to swing through the treetops.

Many animals have amazing feet that have **adapted** over time to their habitat. Some of these animals have four feet, some have two. There are even animals, like the snail, that have only one foot. Imagine that!

Elephants have really big and really amazing feet. Elephants not only use their feet to walk, but also to hear!

5

HANG ON!

Orangutans are the world's largest animals that live in trees. Orangutans' feet have adapted so well to life in the treetops that these animals spend little time on the ground. Smart, strong orangutans are part of the great ape family.

Orangutans use their feet and hands to hold on to branches and vines. They swing through the trees of the rain forest. They use their long toes to hang upside down from a branch while picking fruit.

An orangutan cannot stand with its feet flat on the ground. This is why these apes spend most of their time in the trees.

This baby orangutan is using its feet to hold on to the branch while it munches on some fruit.

BIRDS OF PREY

Hawks are great hunters, and their feet are very important tools. These birds of **prey** use their strong feet to catch their food. Each foot has only four toes, but they are deadly.

A hawk dives down from the sky and lowers its feet to catch small birds or mice. At the end of each toe are long, sharp, curved claws called talons. A hawk can use its powerful feet to squeeze the prey. It can also use its talons to kill its prey before eating it.

A hawk has three toes that point forward and one toe that points backward. This allows it to hold tightly on to branches and its prey.

Turtles are known for being slow. Sea turtles may surprise you, though! Their "feet" are wide **flippers**, which make them strong swimmers and divers. Sea turtles use their front flippers like wings to swim quickly through the water. They use their back flippers to turn and stop.

Flippers are just as important on land as they are in the water. When a mother sea turtle pulls herself onto the beach to lay her eggs, she uses her back flippers to dig her nest. She then uses all her flippers and covers the eggs to hide them from **predators**.

The sea turtle has long bones in its flippers that are like the bones in our hands and feet.

A SNAIL'S PACE

Snails may move slowly but then again, they have only one foot! They use the many **muscles** in the bottom of this foot to crawl.

The snail's foot also makes **mucus**. This sounds kind of gross to you and me, but the snail counts on this mucus to get around. The mucus helps the snail slide along the ground. This same mucus can also be sticky. This gives the snail a strong hold and allows it to climb. When not moving, a snail can pull its foot into its shell. This is one way it stays safe.

The snail's foot is the flat brown part that is spread out on the log. The muscles in the foot are very strong.

SUPER SWIMMERS

Have you ever seen a seal spin and dive in the water? These amazing swimmers are called **pinnipeds**. This means "fin-footed." Seals have four large flippers as feet. They use these flippers to move quickly through the water as they chase and catch fish.

Seals also spend time on land. On land they use their front flippers to crawl. Flippers also have another special job. They help the seal get rid of extra body heat. This lets the seal cool off when its body gets too hot.

Here you can see the fingerlike parts at the end of the flipper. There are small claws at the end, like our fingernails.

Webs are not just for spiders. A duck has webs, too. It has webbed feet! Each foot has one short toe in the back and three long toes in the front with skin between them.

A duck uses its feet to paddle through the water while it searches for food. These webbed feet are what make ducks great swimmers. Having webbed feet also helps ducks walk in the mud. Did you know that these water birds have no **nerves** in their feet, though? This means that their feet never feel cold, no matter how chilly the water gets. Lucky ducks!

Ducks have three toes on their feet. The webbing is the thin skin that is between each toe, as seen here.

CRABBY CLAWS

When most people think of crabs, they likely think of sandy beaches and salty water. Not all crabs live in salt water, though. Some live in freshwater. Some live on land. A few even climb trees. No matter where they live, all crabs have special feet.

Crabs have claws on their two front legs. These claws are used to catch food and tear it into pieces. Sometimes one claw is bigger than the other. Claws are also used to fight. If a crab loses a leg in a fight, it can grow a new one in its place.

You can see the many parts that make up a crab's legs here. This crab has small red claws on the end of its front legs.

FROG FEET

A flying tree frog jumps into the air, spreads its webbed toes, and **glides** from branch to branch. The frog does this to find food. It also uses its special feet to glide away from predators.

There are many kinds of frogs, all with different feet. Frogs that swim use the webbing between their toes to push through water. Frogs that climb have toe pads. These pads have small bumps that help the frog stick to leaves and wet rocks. There are even frogs that dig using a sharp edge on their feet, like a shovel. Now those are some amazing feet!

This is a fire-bellied toad, which likes to live in the water. Its bright colors tell predators that they should leave this frog alone, or they could get sick.

NOT JUST FOR WALKING

Before you learned about what animals' feet can do, you might have thought that animals use their feet only to walk or run. Now you know that this is not true. Over time, some animals' feet have become special tools that help keep them alive. They are important for catching food. They are needed to keep the animal safe. They are necessary for moving and climbing.

There are many different ways feet are used. They can be used in water, in trees, or on land. So many animals have amazing feet. Can you think of some more?

GLOSSARY

adapted (uh-DAPT-ed) Changed to fit new requirements.

features (FEE-churz) The special look or form of a person, an animal, or an object.

flippers (FLIH-perz) Wide, flat body parts that help animals like sea turtles swim.

glides (GLYDZ) Falls freely through the air without flying.

habitats (HA-beh-tats) The kinds of land where animals or plants naturally live.

mucus (MYOO-kus) Thick, slimy matter made by the bodies of many animals.

muscles (MUH-sulz) Parts of the body that make the body move.

nerves (NERVZ) Bunches of fibers that carry messages beweeen the brain and other parts of the body.

pinnipeds (PIH-nuh-pedz) A group of animals, including seals, that have flippers instead of legs.

predators (PREH-duh-terz) Animals that kill other animals for food.

prey (PRAY) An animal that is hunted by another animal for food.

webbed (WEBD) Having skin between the toes, as do ducks, frogs, and other animals that swim.

INDEX

WEB SITES

Due to the changing nature of Internet links, PowerKids Press has developed an online list of Web sites related to the subject of this book. This site is updated regularly. Please use this link to access the list:

www.powerkidslinks.com/cfeat/feet/